Table of Contents

W9-BHT-783

Play With Me
Imagine you are eating breakfast with Elmo. What would you choose to eat?

Shortnin' Bread

Mama's little baby loves shortnin', shortnin',
Mama's little baby loves shortnin' bread.
Mama's little baby loves shortnin', shortnin',
Mama's little baby loves shortnin' bread.

Pease Porridge Hot

Pease porridge hot,
Pease porridge cold,
Pease porridge in the pot,
Nine days old.
Pease porridge hot,
Pease porridge cold,
Pease porridge in the pot,
Nine days old.

Polly, Put the Kettle On

Polly, put the kettle on.
Polly, put the kettle on.
Polly, put the kettle on.
  We'll all have tea.

Play With Me

Banana pancakes are one
of Prairie Dawn's favorite
breakfast foods. Pour some
pretend batter and pat a
pancake for Prairie Dawn.

Pat-a-Cake

Pat-a-cake, pat-a-cake, baker's man,
  Bake me a cake as fast as you can.
Pat it and shape it and mark it with "B,"
  And put it in the oven for baby and me.

Good Morning to You

Good morning to you.
Good morning to you.
  Good morning, dear children.
Good morning to you.

Play With Me
Try greeting all
your favorite toys
with a friendly
"Good morning!"

4

Rig-a-Jig-Jig

Rig-a-jig-jig and away we go,
Away we go, away we go,
Rig-a-jig-jig and away we go,
Heigh-ho, heigh-ho, heigh-ho.

Play With Me

Can you show Elmo how you brush your teeth? Make sure you brush them all!

5

Play With Me
Pretend you're riding
on a bouncy bus.
Bounce as the wheels
go round and round.

The Wheels on the Bus
The wheels on the bus go round and round,
　Round and round, round and round.
The wheels on the bus go round and round,
　All through the town!

Play With Me
Hold hands with a
friend and sing this
song as you spin
around in a circle.

Here We Go Round the Mulberry Bush
Here we go round the mulberry bush,
　The mulberry bush, the mulberry bush.
Here we go round the mulberry bush,
　So early in the morning.

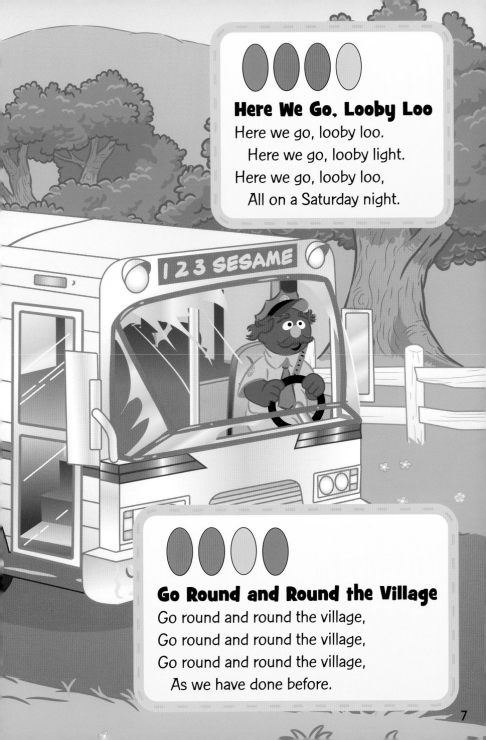

Here We Go, Looby Loo

Here we go, looby loo.
  Here we go, looby light.
Here we go, looby loo,
  All on a Saturday night.

Go Round and Round the Village

Go round and round the village,
Go round and round the village,
Go round and round the village,
  As we have done before.

Farmer in the Dell

The farmer in the dell,
The farmer in the dell,
 Heigh-ho, the derry-oh,
The farmer in the dell.

Little Bo Peep

Little Bo Peep has lost her sheep
 And can't tell where to find them.
Leave them alone and they'll come home,
 Wagging their tails behind them.

Baa, Baa, Black Sheep

Baa, baa, black sheep, have you any wool?
 Yes, sir, yes, sir, three bags full.
One for the master and one for the dame,
 And one for the little boy who lives
 down the lane.

Play With Me
Move around and
make the sounds
your favorite farm
animals make.

Mary Had a Little Lamb

Mary had a little lamb,
  Little lamb, little lamb.
Mary had a little lamb,
  Whose fleece was white as snow.

Animal Fair

I went to the animal fair,
   The birds and the beasts were there,
The big baboon, by the light of the moon,
   Was combing his auburn hair.

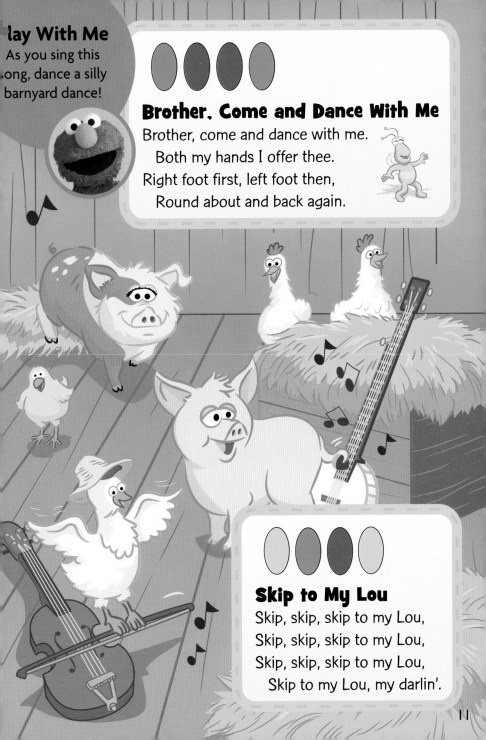

Brother, Come and Dance With Me

Brother, come and dance with me.
Both my hands I offer thee.
Right foot first, left foot then,
Round about and back again.

Skip to My Lou

Skip, skip, skip to my Lou,
Skip, skip, skip to my Lou,
Skip, skip, skip to my Lou,
Skip to my Lou, my darlin'.

Old MacDonald

Old MacDonald had a farm, E-I-E-I-O.
  And on that farm he had some chicks, E-I-E-I-O.
With a peep-peep here, and a peep-peep there,
  Here a peep, there a peep,
Everywhere a peep-peep.
  Old MacDonald had a farm, E-I-E-I-O.

Play With Me
Pretend to plant a seed in the ground and water it. Then watch it grow up, up, up!

Oats, Peas, Beans, and Barley Grow

Oats, peas, beans, and barley grow.

Oats, peas, beans, and barley grow.

Can you or I or anyone know

How oats, peas, beans, and barley grow?

Girls and Boys, Come Out to Play

Girls and boys, come out to play,
   The moon is shining as bright as day.
Leave your supper and leave your sleep,
   And come to your playfellows in the street.

The Green Grass Grew All Around

Now in a hole (now in a hole),
  There was a tree (there was a tree),
The prettiest tree (the prettiest tree),
  That you ever did see (that you ever did see).
The tree in a hole, and the hole in the ground,
  And the green grass grew all around, all around,
And the green grass grew all around.

Play With Me

It's time for a seventh-inning stretch. Stand up, touch your toes, and then reach for the sky!

Take Me Out to the Ball Game

Take me out to the ball game,
  Take me out to the crowd.
Buy me some peanuts and Cracker Jack®,
  I don't care if I never get back.
Let me root, root, root, for the home team,
  If they don't win it's a shame.
For it's one, two, three strikes you're out,
  At the old ball game.

Cracker Jack® is a registered trademark of Frito-Lay.

If You're Happy and You Know It

If you're happy and you know it, clap your hands.
If you're happy and you know it, clap your hands.
   If you're happy and you know it,
Then your face will surely show it.
   If you're happy and you know it, clap your hands.

Play With Me

Can you snap your fingers or stomp your feet? Make up more verses for this song.

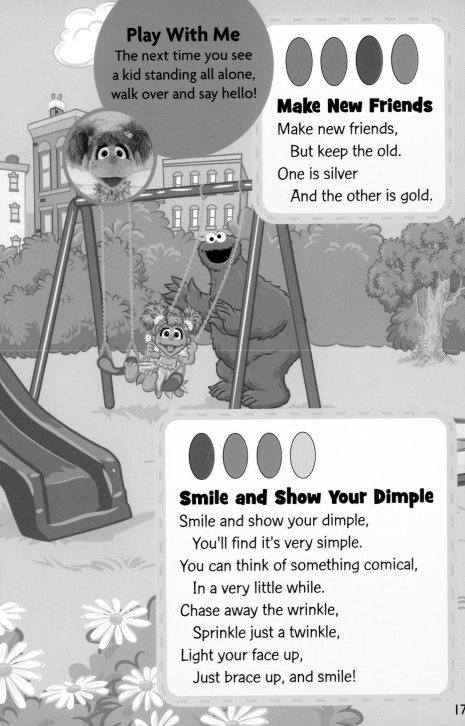

Play With Me

The next time you see
a kid standing all alone,
walk over and say hello!

Make New Friends

Make new friends,
  But keep the old.
One is silver
  And the other is gold.

Smile and Show Your Dimple

Smile and show your dimple,
  You'll find it's very simple.
You can think of something comical,
  In a very little while.
Chase away the wrinkle,
  Sprinkle just a twinkle,
Light your face up,
  Just brace up, and smile!

Play With Me
Next time you take a bath, sing "rub-a-dub-dub" as you scrub, scrub, scrub!

Be Kind to Your Web-Footed Friends

Be kind to your web-footed friends,
  For a duck may be somebody's mother.
Be kind to your friends in the swamp,
  Where the weather is always damp.

Where, Oh Where Has My Little Dog Gone?

Oh where, oh where has my little dog gone?
Oh where, oh where can he be?
With his ears cut short and his tail cut long,
Oh where, oh where can he be?

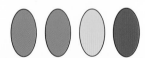

Play With Me
Imagine you are taking care of a pet. What does the pet need to be happy?

Do Your Ears Hang Low?

Do your ears hang low?
Do they wobble to and fro?
Can you tie 'em in a knot?
Can you tie 'em in a bow?
Can you throw 'em over your shoulder,
Like a Continental soldier?
Do your ears hang low?

Head and Shoulders, Knees and Toes

Head and shoulders, knees and toes,
   Knees and toes.
Head and shoulders, knees and toes,
   Knees and toes.
My eyes and ears and mouth and nose,
   Head and shoulders, knees and toes,
Knees and toes.

One, Two, Buckle My Shoe

One, two, buckle my shoe.
   Three, four, knock at the door.
Five, six, pick up sticks.
   Seven, eight, lay them straight.
Nine, ten, do it again.

Ring Around the Rosy

Ring around the rosy,
  A pocket full of posies.
Ashes, ashes,
  We all fall down.

Play With Me

Dance in a circle as you sing this song. When you hear the word "down," drop to the floor. Then get back up and dance in a circle again!

Camptown Races

Camptown ladies sing this song,
  Doo-dah, doo-dah.
Camptown racetrack's five miles long,
  Oh, the doo-dah day.

Jack and Jill

Jack and Jill went up the hill
 To fetch a pail of water.
Jack fell down and broke his crown,
 And Jill came tumbling after.

Polly-Wolly-Doodle

Oh, I went down South for to see my Sal,
 Sing Polly-Wolly-Doodle all the day.
My Sal she is a spunky gal,
 Sing Polly-Wolly-Doodle all the day.

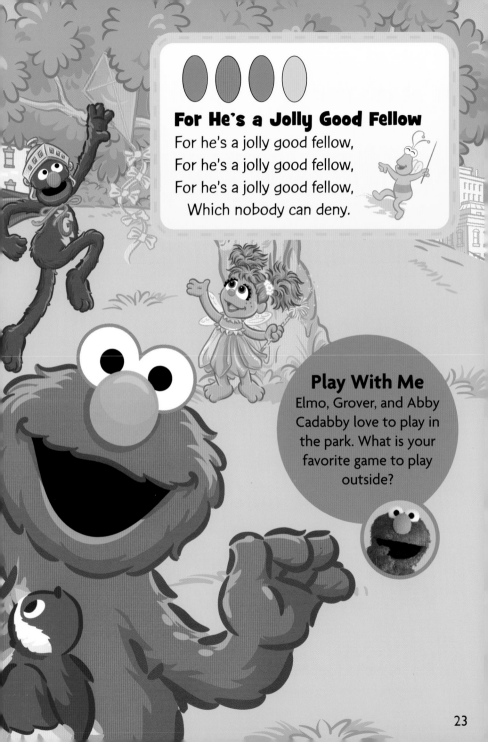

For He's a Jolly Good Fellow

For he's a jolly good fellow,
For he's a jolly good fellow,
For he's a jolly good fellow,
Which nobody can deny.

Play With Me

Elmo, Grover, and Abby Cadabby love to play in the park. What is your favorite game to play outside?

The Band Played On

Casey would waltz with the strawberry blonde,
   And the band played on.
He'd glide 'cross the floor with the girl he adored,
   And the band played on.

Play With Me

Play along on a drum you make yourself. Turn a box or cooking pot upside-down and tap it with a spoon!

Boom, Boom, Ain't It Great to Be Crazy?

Boom, boom, ain't it great to be crazy?
   Boom, boom, ain't it great to be nuts like us?
Silly and foolish all day long,
   Boom, boom, ain't it great to be crazy?

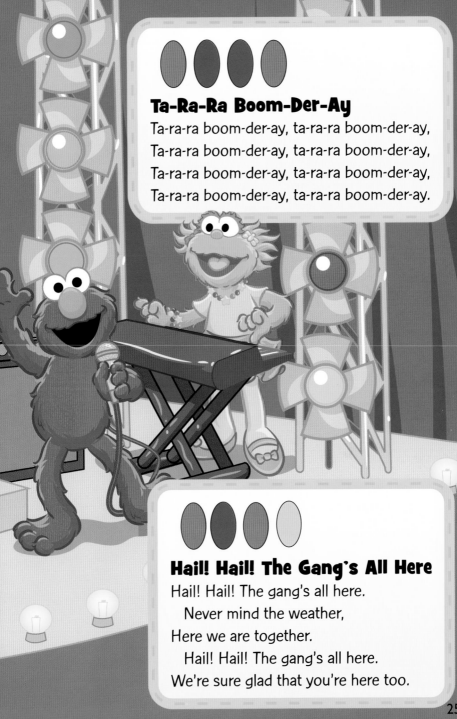

Ta-Ra-Ra Boom-Der-Ay

Ta-ra-ra boom-der-ay, ta-ra-ra boom-der-ay,
Ta-ra-ra boom-der-ay, ta-ra-ra boom-der-ay,
Ta-ra-ra boom-der-ay, ta-ra-ra boom-der-ay,
Ta-ra-ra boom-der-ay, ta-ra-ra boom-der-ay.

Hail! Hail! The Gang's All Here

Hail! Hail! The gang's all here.
  Never mind the weather,
Here we are together.
  Hail! Hail! The gang's all here.
We're sure glad that you're here too.

This Old Man

This old man, he played one,
  He played knick-knack on his thumb.
With a knick-knack paddy whack,
  Give a dog a bone,
This old man came rolling home.

Play With Me
Hide three things somewhere safe and ask a friend to try to find them!

Three Little Kittens

Three little kittens, they lost their mittens,
  And they began to cry,
Oh, mother dear, we sadly fear,
  Our mittens we have lost.
What, lost your mittens? You naughty kittens!
  Then you shall have no pie.

Home Sweet Home

'Mid pleasures and palaces though we may roam,
　Be it ever so humble,
There's no place like home.

Play With Me

What do you like about your home? Think of at least five things.

I See the Moon

I see the moon,
And the moon sees me.
The moon sees the somebody
I'd like to see.

Play With Me

On a starry night, look
out your window. Find
your favorite star in the
sky and make a wish!